Journey through the mysteries of time and space with **"Amazing and Fascinating Fun Facts About Time Traveling!"** This captivating quiz and fact book is perfect for curious kids and teens eager to explore the wonders of time travel, relativity, quantum mechanics, and the universe's greatest secrets. Discover how the fabric of time bends, how clocks slow down in space, and what lies beyond the black holes in a book that brings science to life in an exciting and engaging way.

What's Inside?

- **A Tale of Stars and Time's Dance**: Explore the captivating dance of stars and the flow of time across the cosmos. Uncover how the vastness of space affects time itself and how our understanding of the universe has evolved.

- **The Magic of Relativity Unveiled**: Dive into the world of Einstein's relativity, where the speed of light holds the key to time travel and the mysteries of the cosmos are unlocked. Learn how time can slow down and speed up, and what this means for the future of space exploration.

- **When Clocks Slow Down in Space:** Ever wondered why astronauts age more slowly in space? Discover the fascinating phenomenon of time dilation and what happens to time when you travel at the speed of light.

- **Curves in the Cosmic Playground:** Explore how the fabric of space and time is curved by massive objects like stars and planets. Understand the concepts of gravity, black holes, and the cosmic playground where the universe's most exciting events unfold.

- **Wormholes and Black Holes, Secrets Untold:** Enter the mysterious world of wormholes and black holes, where space and time twist and turn. Could wormholes be the key to time travel? What really happens inside a black hole? Find out in this thrilling chapter!

- **Quantum Mechanics, Mysteries Unfold:** Take a peek into the quantum realm, where particles behave in the most surprising ways. Learn about the bizarre and exciting world of quantum mechanics, where the rules of time and space don't always apply.

- **Parallel Universes, Worlds So Bold:** What if there were other universes just like ours? Dive into the mind-bending concept of parallel universes and explore the possibilities of worlds that exist alongside our own.

- **Paradoxes and Possibilities in Time's Tapestry:** Time travel is full of paradoxes! Learn about the famous grandfather paradox, the butterfly effect, and other mind-boggling scenarios that make time travel so fascinating.

- **Light's Magical Electromagnetism:** Uncover the secrets of light and its incredible journey across the universe. Learn how light behaves, how it can bend time, and why it's essential for understanding the cosmos.

- **The Big Bang's Big Bang Beginning:** Travel back to the beginning of time and explore the Big Bang, the event that created our universe. Learn about the explosive birth of the cosmos and how it set everything in motion.

- **Supernovae: Fireworks in the Sky:** Discover the spectacular explosions of supernovae, the fiery deaths of stars, and how they scatter the elements that make up our universe. Witness the stunning beauty and immense power of these cosmic fireworks.

Why You'll Love This Book

- **Interactive Quizzes**: Each chapter begins with a quiz to challenge your knowledge, followed by detailed answers and fun facts that will spark your imagination and deepen your understanding of time and space.

- **Educational and Fun**: Perfect for kids and teens who love science, space, and the idea of time travel. This book turns complex concepts into fun and accessible knowledge that will entertain and educate.

- **Visually Engaging**: Filled with eye-catching illustrations that bring the wonders of the universe to life, making it easier for young readers to grasp and enjoy.

- **Great for All Ages**: Whether you're a curious kid, a teenager with a passion for science, or an adult looking to learn something new, this book is a perfect companion for anyone interested in the mysteries of time and space.

Best Ways to Use This Book

- **Classroom Adventures:** Teachers can use this book to introduce students to the exciting world of physics, time travel, and the universe. The quizzes and fun facts make learning engaging and interactive.

- **Science Club Favorite:** This book is an excellent resource for science clubs or study groups. Dive into discussions about time travel, quantum mechanics, and the possibilities of the universe.

- **Bedtime Stories with a Twist:** Turn bedtime into a time-traveling adventure! Read a chapter each night and let your child's imagination soar through the stars.

- **Perfect Travel Companion:** Take this book on your next journey through the skies, whether you're traveling across the world or just exploring the wonders of your backyard.

Explore the Mysteries of Time and Space!

With **"Amazing and Fascinating Fun Facts About Time Traveling,"** your child will embark on a mind-expanding journey through the universe. This book is a gateway to understanding the science of time, the cosmos, and the endless possibilities that lie ahead.

Ignite a Passion for Science and Discovery!

Let your child's curiosity lead the way as they explore the fascinating world of time travel and the mysteries of the universe.

Legal Notice

This book is intended for educational and entertainment purposes only. The information provided herein is accurate and true to the best of the author's knowledge, but there may be errors, omissions, or inaccuracies. The author and publisher disclaim any liability in connection with the use of this book.

A Tale of Stars and Time's Dance

Quiz Question

1. What is the name of our galaxy?

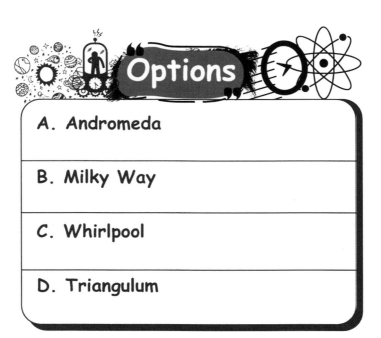

Options

A. Andromeda

B. Milky Way

C. Whirlpool

D. Triangulum

B. Milky Way

Our galaxy is called the Milky Way. It appears as a milky band of light in the night sky, made up of billions of stars. It's a barred spiral galaxy, with our solar system located in one of its spiral arms. This galaxy is vast, and it takes about 100,000 years for light to travel from one end to the other.

• • • • • • • • • • • • •

DID YOU KNOW? **Fun Fact:** If you could travel at the speed of light, it would take you about 100,000 years to cross the Milky Way from one side to the other!

A Tale of Stars and Time's Dance

Quiz Question

2. What keeps planets in orbit around the sun?

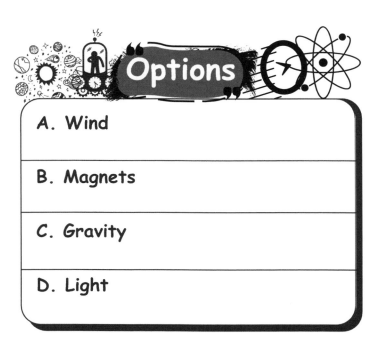

Options

A. Wind

B. Magnets

C. Gravity

D. Light

C. Gravity

Gravity is the force that keeps planets in orbit around the sun. The sun's massive size and gravitational pull attract the planets, holding them in their paths. This gravitational force is invisible, but it's incredibly powerful, guiding the motion of planets, moons, and even comets.

• • • • • • • • • • • • •

Fun Fact: Without gravity, we would all
DID YOU KNOW? float away into space!

A Tale of Stars and Time's Dance

Quiz Question

3. How long does it take the Earth to orbit the sun?

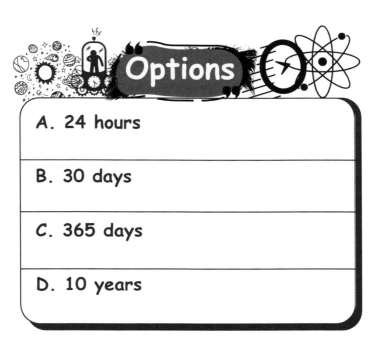

Options

A. 24 hours
B. 30 days
C. 365 days
D. 10 years

C. 365 days

It takes the Earth 365 days, or one year, to complete one orbit around the sun. This journey is called a revolution. The Earth's orbit is slightly elliptical, meaning it's not a perfect circle, but this doesn't affect the length of our year significantly.

· · · · · · · · · · · · ·

DID YOU KNOW? Fun Fact: Every four years, we add an extra day called a leap day to keep our calendar in sync with Earth's orbit!

A Tale of Stars and Time's Dance

Quiz Question

4. What is a black hole?

Options

A. A huge storm
B. An invisible space phenomenon
C. A star explosion
D. A type of planet

B. An invisible space phenomenon

A black hole is an invisible space phenomenon with a gravitational pull so strong that nothing, not even light, can escape from it. Black holes are formed when massive stars collapse under their own gravity. They're mysterious and fascinating, often found at the centers of galaxies.

• • • • • • • • • • • • •

DID YOU KNOW? Fun Fact: The nearest black hole to Earth is about 1,000 light years away in the constellation Monoceros.

A Tale of Stars and Time's Dance

Quiz Question

5. What is the closest star to Earth?

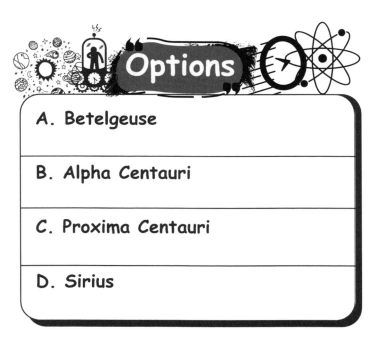

Options

A. Betelgeuse

B. Alpha Centauri

C. Proxima Centauri

D. Sirius

C. Proxima Centauri

Proxima Centauri is the closest star to Earth, located just over four light-years away. It's part of the Alpha Centauri star system and is much smaller and cooler than our sun. Despite its proximity, Proxima Centauri is too faint to be seen with the naked eye.

• • • • • • • • • • • • •

DID YOU KNOW? Fun Fact: If you could travel at the speed of light, it would still take you over four years to reach Proxima Centauri!

Quiz Question

6. What is the fabric of the universe that combines space and time called?

Options

A. Quantum field
B. Space-time continuum
C. Gravitational field
D. Electromagnetic field

B. Space-time continuum

The space-time continuum is a concept that combines the three dimensions of space and the one dimension of time into a single four-dimensional fabric. According to General Relativity, the presence of mass and energy warps this fabric, creating the gravitational effects we observe. This idea fundamentally changed our understanding of the universe.

• • • • • • • • • • • • •

DID YOU KNOW? Fun Fact: The bending of spacetime by massive objects can cause time to pass more slowly near them, an effect known as time dilation!

Quiz Question

7. What phenomenon occurs when light bends around a massive object?

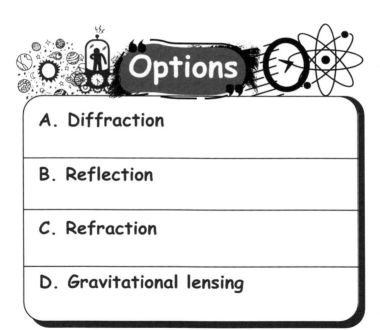

Options

A. Diffraction
B. Reflection
C. Refraction
D. Gravitational lensing

D. Gravitational lensing

Gravitational lensing occurs when a massive object, like a galaxy or black hole, bends the light from objects behind it due to the curvature of spacetime. This effect can magnify and distort the appearance of distant objects, helping astronomers study the universe's structure and distant phenomena.

• • • • • • • • • • • • •

DID YOU KNOW? Fun Fact: Gravitational lensing has enabled the discovery of exoplanets and distant galaxies otherwise too faint to see!

A Tale of Stars and Time's Dance

Quiz Question

8. What is a singularity in space-time?

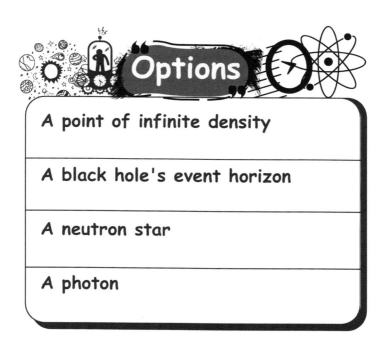

Options

A point of infinite density
A black hole's event horizon
A neutron star
A photon

A. A point of infinite density

A singularity is a point in spacetime where density becomes infinite and the laws of physics as we know them break down. Singularities are found at the centers of black holes, where the gravitational pull is so strong that not even light can escape. They represent some of the most mysterious and extreme conditions in the universe.

• • • • • • • • • • • • •

 Fun Fact: The singularity at the center of a

DID YOU KNOW? black hole has such strong gravity that it warps spacetime to an extreme degree!

The Magic of Relativity Unveiled

Quiz Question

1. Who proposed the theory of relativity?

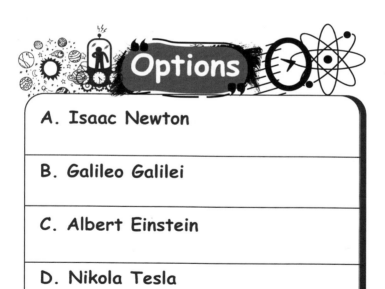

Options

A. Isaac Newton	
B. Galileo Galilei	
C. Albert Einstein	
D. Nikola Tesla	

C. Albert Einstein

Albert Einstein proposed the theory of relativity, which revolutionized our understanding of space and time. His famous equation, $E=mc^2$, shows how energy and mass are interchangeable. The theory of relativity includes special relativity and general relativity and has had profound implications on how we understand the universe.

• • • • • • • ● ● ● • • • •

Fun Fact: Einstein's brain was preserved
DID YOU KNOW? after his death for scientific research!

The Magic of Relativity Unveiled

Quiz Question

2. What is a key concept of special relativity?

Options

A. Constant speed of light
B. Fixed space
C. Static time
D. Immovable objects

A. Constant speed of light

A key concept of special relativity is that the speed of light is constant and is the same for all observers, regardless of their motion. This idea challenges our everyday perceptions of time and space and leads to phenomena like time dilation.

• • • • • • • • • • • • •

DID YOU KNOW? Fun Fact: The speed of light is about 299,792 kilometers per second (186,282 miles per second)!

The Magic of Relativity Unveiled

3. How does relativity affect time?

Options

A. Time speeds up
B. Time stops
C. Time slows down
D. Time changes direction

C. Time slows down

According to relativity, time slows down as you move faster, especially near the speed of light. This effect, called time dilation, means that a fast-moving clock ticks more slowly compared to a stationary one. It's a fascinating concept that has been confirmed by many experiments.

• • • • • • • • • • • •

DID YOU KNOW? Fun Fact: Astronauts aboard the International Space Station experience time slightly slower than people on Earth!

The Magic of Relativity Unveiled

4. What is spacetime?

Options

A. A new planet
B. A type of clock
C. A four-dimensional fabric
D. A space station

C. A four-dimensional fabric

Spacetime is a four-dimensional fabric that combines the three dimensions of space with the fourth dimension of time. This concept, introduced by Einstein, shows how space and time are interconnected and how massive objects can curve spacetime, affecting the motion of other objects.

• • • • • • • • • • • •

DID YOU KNOW? Fun Fact: Spacetime curvature is what makes orbits of planets around stars possible!

The Magic of Relativity Unveiled

Quiz Question

5. What happens to time in a strong gravitational field?

Options

| A. Time speeds up |
| B. Time stands still |
| C. Time moves in reverse |
| D. Time slows down |

D. Time slows down

In a strong gravitational field, time slows down. This effect is known as gravitational time dilation. The stronger the gravity, the slower time passes. This has been observed near massive objects like black holes and even on Earth, where time runs slightly slower at sea level than on a mountain.

• • • • • • • • • • • • •

Fun Fact: GPS satellites must account for
DID YOU KNOW? gravitational time dilation to provide accurate positioning!

Quiz Question

6. What does Einstein's theory of relativity say about time?

Options

A. Time is constant everywhere
B. Time speeds up near massive objects
C. Time slows down near massive objects
D. Time is an illusion

C. Time slows down near massive objects

According to Einstein's theory of relativity, time is not the same everywhere. When you are near a massive object, like a planet or a star, time actually slows down! This means if you lived near a huge star, you'd age more slowly compared to someone far away from it. This phenomenon is known as "time dilation." It's a strange but true effect of Einstein's groundbreaking work on how gravity affects time.

• • • • • • • • • • • •

DID YOU KNOW? Fun Fact: Astronauts age slightly slower in space because they are farther from Earth's gravitational pull!

The Magic of Relativity Unveiled

Quiz Question

7. What kind of object did Einstein use to explain the theory of relativity?

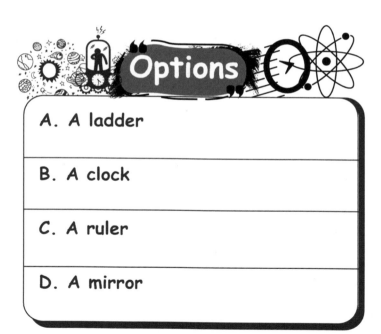

Options

A. A ladder

B. A clock

C. A ruler

D. A mirror

B. A clock

Einstein often used the example of clocks to explain his theory of relativity. Imagine two clocks: if one is closer to a massive object (like Earth), it will tick more slowly compared to one that is farther away. This difference in ticking speed shows how gravity can warp time, an idea that was revolutionary and changed how we understand the universe.

• • • • • • • • • • • •

Fun Fact: Einstein's theories help GPS

DID YOU KNOW? satellites keep accurate time so they can help you find your way!

The Magic of Relativity Unveiled

Quiz Question

8. What happens to time in a moving spaceship according to Einstein's theory?

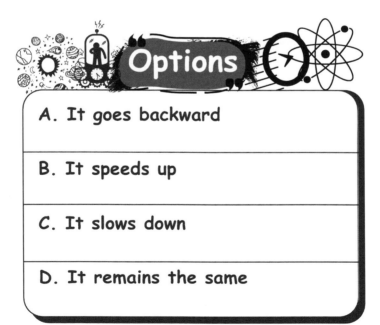

Options

| A. It goes backward |
| B. It speeds up |
| C. It slows down |
| D. It remains the same |

C. It slows down

According to Einstein's theory, if you were traveling in a fast-moving spaceship, time would actually slow down for you compared to people on Earth. This effect is called "time dilation." So, an astronaut traveling at high speeds would age more slowly than their friends and family back on Earth. It's like having a superpower that lets you travel into the future!

• • • • • • • ● ● ● ● • • •

DID YOU KNOW? Fun Fact: If you could travel at the speed of light, you would experience no passage of time at all!

The Magic of Relativity Unveiled

Quiz Question

9. What is the name of the famous equation Einstein formulated?

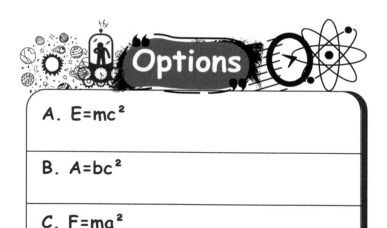

Options

A. E=mc²

B. A=bc²

C. F=ma²

D. G=vr²

A. E=mc²

Einstein's famous equation E=mc² shows how energy (E) and mass (m) are related. According to this equation, mass can be converted into energy and vice versa. This discovery had a huge impact on science, explaining everything from the energy produced by the sun to the potential of nuclear power. It's one of the most well-known equations in the world!

• • • • • • • • • • • •

Fun Fact: The equation E=mc² helped **DID YOU KNOW?** scientists understand how stars shine by converting mass into energy!

Quiz Question

10. What is the name of the phenomenon where time slows down near a massive object?

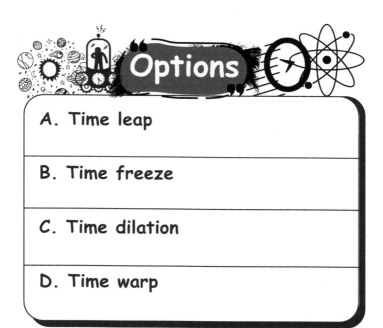

Options

A. Time leap

B. Time freeze

C. Time dilation

D. Time warp

C. Time dilation

Time dilation is the phenomenon where time slows down near a massive object, like a planet or a star. This happens because gravity affects time, making clocks tick more slowly in strong gravitational fields. It's one of the amazing predictions of Einstein's theory of relativity and has been confirmed by many experiments. It shows just how strange and wonderful our universe is!

• • • • • • • ● ● ● • • • •

DID YOU KNOW? Fun Fact: Time dilation has been confirmed by flying atomic clocks on airplanes and comparing them to clocks on the ground!

The Magic of Relativity Unveiled

Quiz Question

11. What does a "tachyon" supposedly do?

Options

| A. Travel faster than light |
| B. Bend space |
| C. Slow down time |
| D. Create black holes |

A. Travel faster than light

A tachyon is a hypothetical particle that is theorized to travel faster than the speed of light. According to Einstein's theory of relativity, nothing can travel faster than light, but tachyons are a curious exception in theoretical physics. If tachyons exist, they could offer new insights into the nature of time and space, and potentially open up possibilities for time travel.

• • • • • • • • • • • •

Quiz Question

12. Who is famous for black hole research and wrote "A Brief History of Time"?

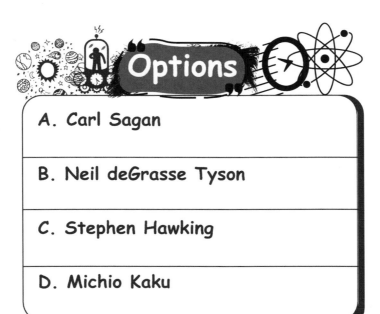

Options

A. Carl Sagan
B. Neil deGrasse Tyson
C. Stephen Hawking
D. Michio Kaku

C. Stephen Hawking

Stephen Hawking was a renowned physicist known for his groundbreaking research on black holes and his popular science book "A Brief History of Time." Hawking's work helped us understand phenomena like black hole radiation and the nature of the universe. Despite his physical challenges, he made significant contributions to science and inspired countless people to explore the wonders of the cosmos.

• • • • • • • • • • • •

DID YOU KNOW? Fun Fact: Stephen Hawking's voice synthesizer, which he used to communicate, became one of the most recognizable voices in the world!

When Clocks Slow Down in Space

Quiz Question

1. What is time dilation?

Options

A. Time stopping
B. Time speeding up
C. Time being distorted
D. Time moving in circles

C. Time being distorted

Time dilation is the phenomenon where time appears to be distorted due to the relative motion between observers or the presence of strong gravitational fields. It means that a clock moving at high speeds or near a massive object will tick more slowly compared to a stationary clock.

• • • • • • • • • • • •

DID YOU KNOW? Fun Fact: If you travel at 99% the speed of light, time would slow down for you so much that you could travel to a star 4 light-years away and back in just over a year, according to your watch!

When Clocks Slow Down in Space

Quiz Question

2. Why do astronauts experience time differently in space?

Options

| A. They travel fast |
| B. They sleep less |
| C. They eat special food |
| D. They are closer to the stars |

A. They travel fast

Astronauts experience time differently in space because they travel at high speeds. According to Einstein's theory of relativity, as their speed increases, time slows down for them compared to people on Earth. This effect, though very small, can be measured with precise clocks.

• • • • • • • • • • • • •

Fun Fact: Astronauts on the ISS age slightly slower than people on Earth due to their high speed and lower gravity!

DID YOU KNOW?

When Clocks Slow Down in Space

Quiz Question

3. What did the Hafele-Keating experiment prove?

Options

A. Time travel is possible

B. Time dilation is real

C. Space is flat

D. Clocks are unreliable

B. Time dilation is real

The Hafele-Keating experiment involved flying atomic clocks on airplanes around the world and comparing them to stationary clocks. The results showed that the moving clocks experienced time dilation and ran slower, confirming Einstein's predictions.

• • • • • • • • • • • •

DID YOU KNOW? Fun Fact: The atomic clocks used in the Hafele-Keating experiment were accurate to within a billionth of a second!

When Clocks Slow Down in Space

4. How does speed affect time?

Options

A. It makes time faster
B. It has no effect
C. It makes time slower
D. It stops time

C. It makes time slower

As speed increases, time slows down, a concept known as time dilation. This effect becomes more noticeable as the speed approaches the speed of light. It's an amazing consequence of Einstein's theory of relativity that challenges our everyday understanding of time.

• • • • • • • • • • • •

DID YOU KNOW? Fun Fact: If you could travel at the speed of light, time would stand still for you!

Quiz Question

5. Why do GPS satellites need to account for time dilation?

Options

| A. To save energy |
| B. To avoid collisions |
| C. To provide accurate timings |
| D. To stay in orbit |

C. To provide accurate timings

GPS satellites need to account for time dilation to provide accurate positioning. They orbit Earth at high speeds and experience less gravity, causing their clocks to run faster than those on the ground. Corrections are made to ensure the GPS system works correctly.

• • • • • • ● • • • • •

Fun Fact: Without time dilation corrections, **DID YOU KNOW?** GPS errors would accumulate to several kilometers per day!

When Clocks Slow Down in Space

Quiz Question

What happens to time when you travel at speeds close to the speed of light?

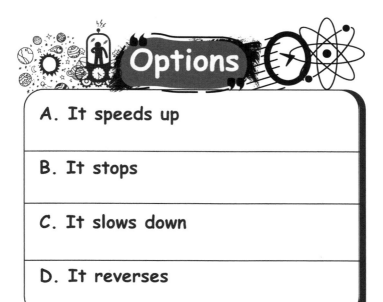

Options

A. It speeds up

B. It stops

C. It slows down

D. It reverses

C. It slows down

When you travel at speeds close to the speed of light, time actually slows down for you compared to people who are not traveling at such speeds. This is another example of time dilation, a fascinating consequence of Einstein's theory of relativity. This means that astronauts traveling on a super-fast spaceship would age more slowly than people on Earth.

• • • • • • • • • • • • •

DID YOU KNOW? Fun Fact: If you could travel at 99% of the speed of light, time would pass about seven times slower for you than for someone on Earth!

Curves in the Cosmic Playground

Quiz Question

1. What does spacetime curvature explain?

Options

A. Why the sky is blue
B. How objects move
C. Why stars twinkle
D. How plants grow

B. How objects move

Spacetime curvature explains how objects move in the presence of gravity. Massive objects like planets and stars curve the fabric of spacetime, creating paths that other objects follow. This curvature guides planets in their orbits and explains phenomena like the bending of light around stars.

• • • • • • • • • • • • •

Fun Fact: The bending of light by gravity is called gravitational lensing and can magnify distant galaxies!

DID YOU KNOW?

Curves in the Cosmic Playground

2. What creates spacetime curvature?

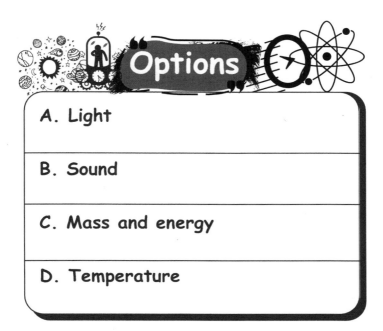

Options

A. Light
B. Sound
C. Mass and energy
D. Temperature

C. Mass and energy

Mass and energy create spacetime curvature. The more massive an object, the greater the curvature it creates. This curvature affects the motion of other objects, bending their paths. Even light is influenced by spacetime curvature, leading to fascinating effects like gravitational lensing.

• • • • • • • • • • • •

Fun Fact: The Earth curves spacetime, which is why objects fall towards the ground!

DID YOU KNOW?

3. What is an example of spacetime curvature we can observe?

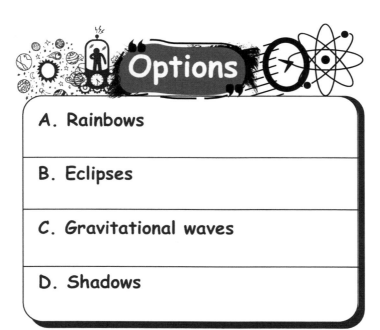

Options

A. Rainbows
B. Eclipses
C. Gravitational waves
D. Shadows

C. Gravitational waves

Gravitational waves are ripples in spacetime curvature, caused by massive objects like merging black holes or neutron stars. These waves travel through space, stretching and compressing it. They were predicted by Einstein and first detected in 2015, confirming a key aspect of general relativity.

• • • • • • ● ● ● ● • • •

Fun Fact: Gravitational waves were detected
DID YOU KNOW? using incredibly sensitive instruments called interferometers!

Curves in the Cosmic Playground

Quiz Question

4. How does the sun's gravity affect the Earth?

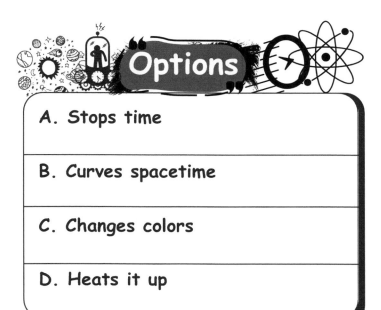

Options

A. Stops time
B. Curves spacetime
C. Changes colors
D. Heats it up

B. Curves spacetime

The sun's gravity curves spacetime around it, creating a gravitational field that holds the Earth in its orbit. This curvature ensures that Earth follows a stable path around the sun, maintaining the conditions necessary for life.

• • • • • • • • • • • •

DID YOU KNOW? Fun Fact: If the sun suddenly disappeared, Earth would continue in a straight line due to the lack of curvature!

Quiz Question

5. What happens to light near a black hole?

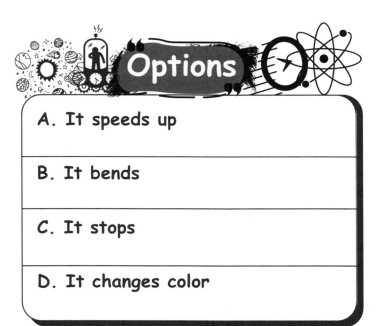

Options

A. It speeds up
B. It bends
C. It stops
D. It changes color

B. It bends

Light bends near a black hole due to the immense curvature of spacetime created by the black hole's gravity. This bending can be so severe that light can orbit the black hole or be trapped, making the black hole appear invisible.

• • • • • • • • • • • •

Fun Fact: The event horizon is the boundary **DID YOU KNOW?** around a black hole beyond which nothing can escape, not even light!

-62-

Wormholes and Black Holes, Secrets Untold

Quiz Question

1. What are wormholes often described as?

Options

A. Tunnels through space
B. Giant whirlpools
C. Supermassive stars
D. Dangerous asteroids

A. Tunnels through space

Wormholes are often depicted as tunnels or shortcuts through space and time, connecting two distant points in the universe. If they exist, they could allow for rapid travel between these points, far faster than light speed. This concept fascinates scientists and science fiction fans alike.

• • • • • • • • • • • •

DID YOU KNOW? Some scientists believe that if wormholes exist, they could potentially allow for time travel, though this remains purely theoretical.

Quiz Question

2. What is at the center of a black hole?

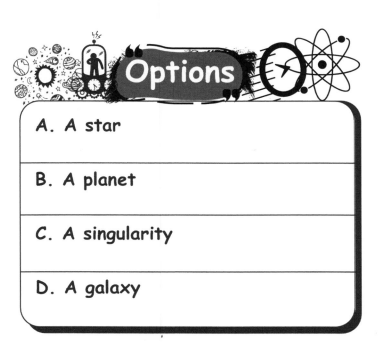

Options

A. A star

B. A planet

C. A singularity

D. A galaxy

C. A singularity

The center of a black hole is called a singularity, where gravity is so strong that it crushes all matter and space-time to an infinite density. It's a point where our current understanding of physics breaks down, making it one of the most mysterious objects in the universe.

• • • • • • • • • • • •

DID YOU KNOW? Black holes are so dense that not even light can escape their gravitational pull, which is why they appear black to observers.

3. What famous scientist predicted the existence of black holes?

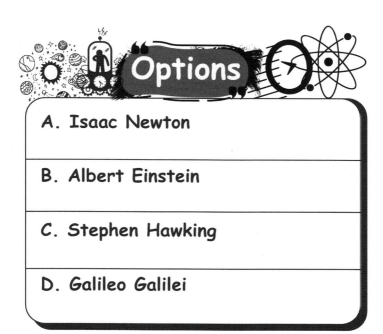

Options

| A. Isaac Newton |
| B. Albert Einstein |
| C. Stephen Hawking |
| D. Galileo Galilei |

B. Albert Einstein

Albert Einstein's theory of general relativity predicted the existence of black holes, even though he himself was skeptical of their existence. It wasn't until later that black holes were confirmed through various observations and studies in astrophysics.

● ● ● ● ● ● ● ● ● ● ● ● ●

DID YOU KNOW? Stephen Hawking later contributed significantly to black hole theory, particularly with his prediction of Hawking radiation.

Quiz Question

4. What term describes the boundary around a black hole from which nothing can escape?

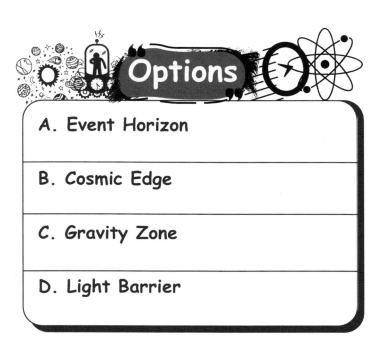

Options

A. Event Horizon
B. Cosmic Edge
C. Gravity Zone
D. Light Barrier

A. Event Horizon

The event horizon is the boundary around a black hole beyond which nothing can escape, not even light. Once an object crosses this boundary, it is pulled inexorably towards the singularity at the center of the black hole, making it disappear from our observable universe.

• • • • • • • • • • • •

DID YOU KNOW? The term "event horizon" was popularized by physicist John Archibald Wheeler, who coined many terms in black hole science.

Quiz Question

5. What is a hypothetical bridge connecting two black holes called?

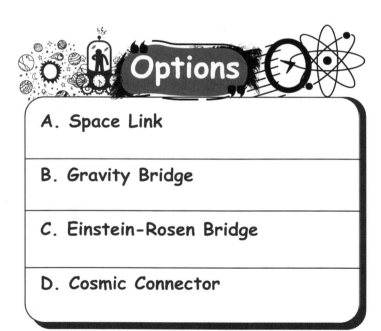

Options

A. Space Link

B. Gravity Bridge

C. Einstein-Rosen Bridge

D. Cosmic Connector

C. Einstein-Rosen Bridge

An Einstein-Rosen Bridge, more commonly known as a wormhole, is a hypothetical bridge that could connect two separate points in space-time. Named after physicists Albert Einstein and Nathan Rosen, this concept suggests a shortcut through the universe, although its existence is still unproven.

• • • • • • • • • • • •

DID YOU KNOW? **The idea of wormholes was first introduced in a paper by Einstein and Rosen in 1935.**

Quiz Question

6. What is a wormhole often compared to?

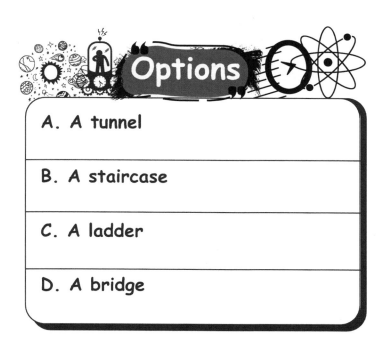

Options

A. A tunnel
B. A staircase
C. A ladder
D. A bridge

A. A tunnel

A wormhole is often compared to a tunnel because it is imagined as a shortcut through spacetime, connecting two distant points with a shorter path. If you could enter a wormhole, you could travel vast distances in a much shorter time than if you traveled through normal space. Wormholes are fascinating theoretical objects predicted by Einstein's equations, though none have been found yet.

· · · · · · ● ● ● ● · · · ·

DID YOU KNOW? Fun Fact: Some scientists think wormholes could allow for time travel, letting you visit the past or future!

Quiz Question

7. What is another name for a wormhole?

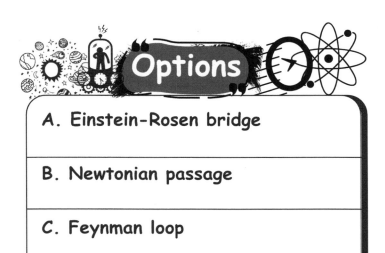

Options

A. Einstein-Rosen bridge

B. Newtonian passage

C. Feynman loop

D. Curie corridor

A. Einstein-Rosen bridge

A wormhole is also known as an Einstein-Rosen bridge, named after physicists Albert Einstein and Nathan Rosen, who first proposed the idea. This fascinating concept suggests a "bridge" that could connect different parts of the universe or even different universes altogether. It's a mind-bending idea that shows just how strange and wonderful the universe could be.

• • • • • • • • • • • • •

Quiz Question

8. What would you need to keep a wormhole open?

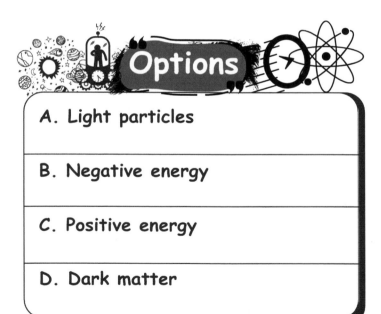

Options

A. Light particles
B. Negative energy
C. Positive energy
D. Dark matter

B. Negative energy

To keep a wormhole open, scientists think you would need a substance called "negative energy." This mysterious and hypothetical form of energy might counteract the forces trying to close the wormhole. While negative energy hasn't been proven to exist, it's a thrilling idea that scientists are still exploring.

• • • • • • ● ● ● ● • • •

Fun Fact: The concept of negative energy **DID YOU KNOW?** comes from quantum physics, a branch of science that studies the tiniest particles in the universe!

Wormholes and Black Holes, Secrets Untold

Quiz Question

9. What is believed to happen if you enter a portal in science fiction?

Options

A. You vanish forever
B. You travel through space
C. You turn into an alien
D. You become invisible

B. You travel through space

In many science fiction stories, entering a portal allows characters to travel instantly to distant places in space or even to different dimensions. Portals are fascinating devices that spark the imagination, making us wonder about the secrets of the universe and the possibilities of instant travel.

• • • • • • • • • • • •

DID YOU KNOW? Fun Fact: The idea of portals has been featured in famous stories like "The Chronicles of Narnia" and movies like "Stargate"!

Quiz Question

10. What scientific theory allows the existence of wormholes?

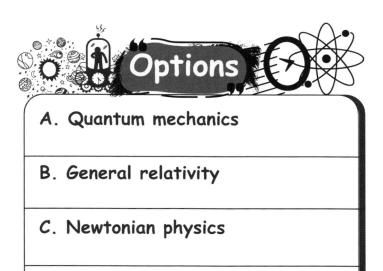

Options

A. Quantum mechanics

B. General relativity

C. Newtonian physics

D. String theory

B. General relativity

The existence of wormholes is allowed by Einstein's theory of general relativity, which describes how gravity works. According to this theory, spacetime can be warped and stretched, making the concept of wormholes possible. Although they remain theoretical, wormholes continue to intrigue scientists and inspire imaginative stories.

• • • • • • • • • • • •

Fun Fact: Wormholes are sometimes called "shortcuts" through spacetime because they could connect two distant points in the universe!

DID YOU KNOW?

Quiz Question

1. What is it called when a particle exists in multiple states at once?

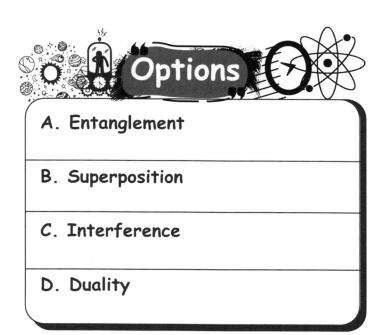

Options

A. Entanglement
B. Superposition
C. Interference
D. Duality

B. Superposition

Superposition is the principle in quantum mechanics where a particle can exist in multiple states simultaneously. For example, an electron can be in multiple places at once until it is observed. This idea is famously illustrated by Schrödinger's cat, a thought experiment involving a cat that can be both alive and dead.

• • • • • • • • • • • • •

 **DID YOU KNOW?** The concept of superposition is fundamental to quantum computing, which uses quantum bits or qubits to perform complex calculations far faster than classical computers.

Quantum Mechanics, Mysteries Unfold

Quiz Question

2. What phenomenon occurs when two particles remain connected over distance?

Options

A. Quantum Leap

B. Quantum Entanglement

C. Quantum Tunneling

D. Quantum State

B. Quantum Entanglement

Quantum entanglement occurs when two particles become connected, so the state of one instantly influences the state of the other, regardless of the distance between them. This "spooky action at a distance," as Einstein called it, challenges our understanding of space and time.

• • • • • • • • • • • •

DID YOU KNOW? Entangled particles have been experimentally verified to communicate faster than the speed of light, defying classical physics.

Quiz Question

3. What term is used for particles passing through a barrier they shouldn't?

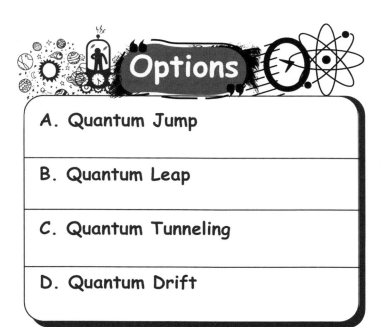

Options

A. Quantum Jump

B. Quantum Leap

C. Quantum Tunneling

D. Quantum Drift

C. Quantum Tunneling

Quantum tunneling describes the phenomenon where particles pass through a barrier that would be insurmountable according to classical physics. This is possible because of the wave-like nature of particles at the quantum level, allowing them to "tunnel" through seemingly solid objects.

• • • • • • • • • • • • •

DID YOU KNOW? Quantum tunneling is essential in nuclear fusion, the process powering stars and potentially future clean energy sources on Earth.

Quiz Question

4. What principle states you can't simultaneously know a particle's exact position and momentum?

Options

A. Uncertainty Principle
B. Relativity Principle
C. Exclusion Principle
D. Equivalence Principle

A. Uncertainty Principle

The Uncertainty Principle, formulated by Werner Heisenberg, states that it is impossible to know both the exact position and momentum of a particle at the same time. The more precisely one is known, the less precisely the other can be known, highlighting the limits of measurement in quantum physics.

• • • • • • • • • • • •

DID YOU KNOW? The Uncertainty Principle is a fundamental aspect of quantum mechanics and has profound implications for our understanding of the microscopic world.

Quantum Mechanics, Mysteries Unfold

Quiz Question

5. What is the smallest unit of energy in quantum mechanics called?

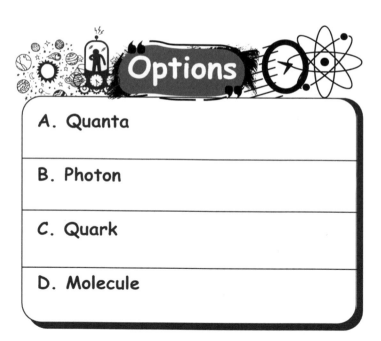

Options

A. Quanta

B. Photon

C. Quark

D. Molecule

A. Quanta

In quantum mechanics, energy is quantized, meaning it comes in small, discrete units called quanta. A quantum is the smallest possible unit of any physical property, such as energy or matter. This concept helps explain why energy levels in atoms and molecules are not continuous, but rather exist in specific steps.

• • • • • • • • • • • •

DID YOU KNOW? The term "quantum" was first used by Max Planck, the father of quantum theory, to describe the discrete nature of energy exchange in atoms.

6. What do we call a particle of light?

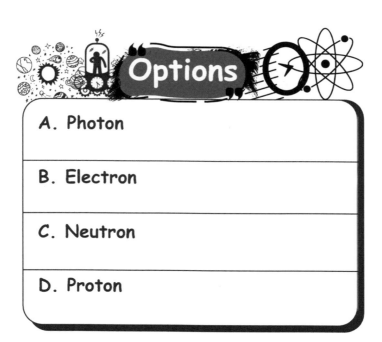

Options

A. Photon
B. Electron
C. Neutron
D. Proton

A. Photon

A photon is the smallest possible unit of light, a tiny packet of energy that travels at the speed of light. Photons don't have mass and can be thought of as both particles and waves, embodying the puzzling and wondrous nature of quantum mechanics. They are essential for vision, photosynthesis, and even solar power.

• • • • • • • • • • • • •

DID YOU KNOW? Fun Fact: Did you know that it takes about 8 minutes for a photon from the Sun to reach Earth?

Quantum Mechanics, Mysteries Unfold

Quiz Question

7. What is the phenomenon where particles are instantly connected, no matter the distance?

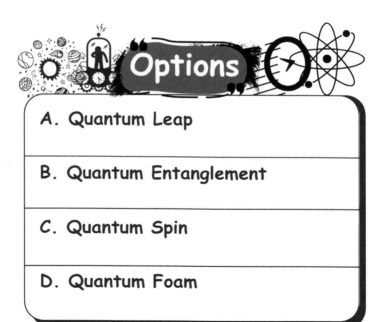

Options

A. Quantum Leap

B. Quantum Entanglement

C. Quantum Spin

D. Quantum Foam

B. Quantum Entanglement

Quantum Entanglement is a magical phenomenon where two particles become intertwined, so the state of one instantly influences the state of the other, regardless of the distance between them. This "spooky action at a distance," as Einstein called it, is a cornerstone of quantum mechanics and could revolutionize communication and computing.

· · · · · · ● ● ● ● ● · · ·

DID YOU KNOW? Fun Fact: Scientists have entangled particles over distances of more than 1,200 kilometers using satellites!

Quiz Question

8. Which principle states that we cannot know both the position and momentum of a particle exactly?

Options

A. Relativity Principle
B. Uncertainty Principle
C. Exclusion Principle
D. Correspondence Principle

B. Uncertainty Principle

The Uncertainty Principle, introduced by Werner Heisenberg, states that it is impossible to know both the exact position and exact momentum of a particle simultaneously. This principle is fundamental in quantum mechanics and signifies that the more precisely we know one quantity, the less precisely we can know the other. It highlights the strange and probabilistic nature of the quantum world.

• • • • • • ● ● ● • • • •

DID YOU KNOW? Fun Fact: The Uncertainty Principle means that the quantum world is inherently unpredictable, which contrasts with our everyday experiences!